PORTAL

PHOENIX POETS

Edited by Srikanth Reddy

Rosa Alcalá, Douglas Kearney &

Katie Peterson, consulting editors

PORTAL

TRACY FUAD

THE UNIVERSITY OF CHICAGO PRESS
CHICAGO & LONDON

The University of Chicago Press, Chicago 60637
The University of Chicago Press, Ltd., London
©2024 by The University of Chicago
Published 2024
Printed in the United States of America

33 32 31 30 29 28 27 26 25 24   1 2 3 4 5

ISBN-13: 978-0-226-83153-4 (paper)
ISBN-13: 978-0-226-83154-1 (e-book)
DOI: https://doi.org/10.7208/chicago/9780226831541.001.0001

Library of Congress Cataloging-in-Publication Data

Names: Fuad, Tracy, author.
Title: Portal / Tracy Fuad.
Other titles: Phoenix poets.
Description: Chicago : The University of Chicago Press, 2024. | Series: Phoenix poets
Identifiers: LCCN 2023036272 | ISBN 9780226831534 (paperback) | ISBN 9780226831541 (ebook)
Subjects: LCGFT: Poetry.
Classification: LCC PS3606.U23 P67 2024 | DDC 811/.6—dc23/eng/20230807
LC record available at https://lccn.loc.gov/2023036272

♾ This paper meets the requirements of ANSI/NISO Z39.48-1992 (Permanence of Paper).

for Marin Orlando, who loves doors

CONTENTS

mortal

    Song 5

    Hyposubject 11

    Hyposubject 12

    Hyposubject 13

    Hyposubject 14

    Hyposubject 15

    Hyposubject 16

    Hyposubject 17

    The Third Space 18

torpor

    Business 24

    Body of Water 2 33

    Vacuum 39

    Zeitgeist 44

    One Thousand Nights 48

mortar, pestle

    The First Planetary Boundary 54

    The Second Planetary Boundary 55

    The Third Planetary Boundary 56

    The Fourth Planetary Boundary 57

    The Fifth Planetary Boundary 58

    The Sixth Planetary Boundary 59

The Seventh Planetary Boundary 60
The Eighth Planetary Boundary 61
The Ninth Planetary Boundary 62
The Tenth Planetary Boundary 63

portal

Radicality 66
Nihilism 68
Destiny 70
Abundance 72
Lunch 80
Alphabet 82
Beach 83
Internet 86
Change 88
Worm 89
Gong 90
Birth 95

Acknowledgments 97

PORTAL

mortal

SONG

Sometimes it was just a humming
Which came through the windows at night
When I couldn't sleep
The sun already warming
The cool air of night
The pitch of the humming
Not unlike
The pitch of the singing
Which came from the couple
Two stories up
Who sang opera
Which came down the walls
Which were thick
Built
It would seem
Out of rubble
Except for the walls
Between rooms
We learned one hot day in July
The point of a screw emerging in our bedroom
From the pentagonal kitchen
Which looked out on the backyard
Where the beans I'd sowed
In mounds of earth
Were brutalized each night
By slugs or snails
Which roamed the plots
Especially after rain
Though it rained so little
The grasses bleaching yellow
Though summer had barely begun
Their bodies as long as fingers
And nearly translucent
Their undulations subtle

And yet
In increments
They crossed the subdivisions
Which we had laid
With brick
In imitation of the squares we lived in
Which shared walls
Through which we heard the neighbors fight
And then make up
And they heard us.
Sometimes I flung the slugs
Over the fence
Remorseless
Other times deciding
It would be cruelty to do so
Even if my flinging meant that briefly
The gastropod would fly
Even with the knowledge they'd return
Would penetrate the chain-link fence
To eat the waxen bean leaves
Young and doomed.
Once I even found a lone slug
In the foyer
And hunched to trace
Its gleaming trail of substance
Showing with precision
The path it had traveled.
A slug is not
As you might think
A snail without a shell
A slug lives its whole life
Without a shell
Like I do
Scurrying across the street to weep
Before the woman singing
Outside the Neukölln Town Hall

Her low clear notes unearthly
In the morning rush
A sort of song
I'd never heard before.
Once it was a melody
I swore I knew
Which entered my apartment
So alluring
That I ran out to the balcony
Then pressed my ear against
The thick walls
Then the thin ones
But heard it clearest
In the middle of my bedroom
As if it was the air itself
That sang.
And still
I make my stale ritual
Each week or so
Logging on my fake account
To watch the stories
Of a lover
From whom I'm estranged
Clicking through three years
To reach the present
Noting the deletion of my presence
Though not the images I filmed of her
Twirling in a crimson cape
As bells rang in the darkness
And in daylight
Spread-armed beside a flooded river
And the inking of a ginkgo leaf
That matches mine
Which we'd driven up to Köln to get
Three years ago last winter
Almost four.

Now I climb in nearly daily
And with utmost caution
To the bathtub
My great windfall
Though it is so small
I need to curl up fetally
To fit in it.
Submerged
I press my fingertips
Against the dome of flesh
I had become
Trying to find the hard sphere
Of the baby's head
Then what the midwife called
The "little pieces"
By which she meant
The baby's feet and hands.
In bed I browsed potential monitors
With convex eyes of glass
To see the baby from a distance
And in darkness
With technology
Developed by the British Army
So in theory
I could watch the baby
While I drank a blood-orange cocktail
Down the street at Neue Republik
Which I'd deemed a needed if symbolic
Return to what I called
My life
The possessive *my*
Essential to the notion
That the sum of what I saw and felt
Belonged to me—
The leaves that fluttered
On the other side of gauze

I'd hung up in my bedroom
And the beam of sun
Which cut through
And revealed the hovering
Motes of dust
For a precise number of minutes
Which varied
In accordance with the season
And the blighted beans
That I had planted
And the bricks
Laid into the street
Where the wall used to stand
Which I followed some mornings
As I walked alone
And the hands and feet
And the toes and fingers
Of my baby
As I saw them for the first time
And the singing—
That all of this
Was mine
Although it wasn't.

HYPOSUBJECT

In life, I imbued things with a great deal of meaning and purpose.

At times, as if possessed.

I waited to understand reason, but it seemed to gather speed and breadth without me, as if reason itself, once seeded, began to breathe and grow on its own.

But officials have said the hole is perfect.

So now I focus on the practical use of the past.

The light of day. A blue chair standing before the mirror.

It occurred to me after the end, the fifth of that week, arriving where the doors were closed: I may have died.

How do you feel when the world is big inside your head?

Another common moment.

HYPOSUBJECT

I hope this button works, but I really can't tell.

Everyday there are more and more portals between people and places.

Verbs, for example, prefer not to live alone like me.

Every year I learn a language.

This way I can better grasp the impact separation.

I had no clue how to hold someone's mouth when they spoke. I found myself reeling.

I'd thought a universal theory would arise eventually if I was able to closely follow the text, color, pattern in the drafts, as well as the more subtle features: fluid, tenor, fragmentation.

I have found myself instead again and again at various ends.

I was so flat. What could hold a thing like me?

I was just fine, washing my fingers. It was my interest.

When the power came back, the radio began to play all on its own.

For me alone, the music.

HYPOSUBJECT

I have a strong experience of skin.

When someone steps out of the room, I can breathe.

As I wash, my blood flows. The little pieces that I go to.

I keep my fingers from what my hands are doing.

I suffer from severe tenderness and sometimes dryness.

I'm afraid one day my skin won't close and I won't be able to use my hands.

So hold, hold, work against the powers of cuts that are missing places and people.

The sadness of objects behind all emotions.

The little that I walked. The principles of foot and forest.

Sorry, the time: I must resume my journey.

HYPOSUBJECT

I tried to convey my dreams into the cold of living by announcement.

I thought that I could think that way.

Are they dangerous to the world, my thoughts of paradise between things?

At times I have nightmares and return.

Hassle and repetition. Commotion and schedule. Hoarding and planning.

My tools stung me, but sometimes they were obvious.

Words have seemed false to me, and sometimes they were.

One night I woke up the whole family by exclaiming, *Look, a pod of orcas!*

Had there been one?

I must find my way to mourn.

HYPOSUBJECT

I had an eternal relationship with myself. A hedonistic ship, but innocent.

At dawn I could make endlessness. And love all night.

However, when I stood to go, I couldn't break into living.

My wishes, loves, and quests were broken as a rule, and bound in half a year.

At times I have the thought that I have used my being wrongly.

I spent my life preparing for my life.

One day I told myself this thing had happened.

I realized that my life would continue.

HYPOSUBJECT

I was always waiting for a phone call, a message; something to connect my phantom days.

I wanted the worst, and so was punished with fantastic vibrations.

In a dream, I saw a brooch of thorns. I saw my unawareness.

I wanted to break the pith inside, but it's gone, and I can't.

I knew to leave a trail of leftovers behind me and behind me.

I was consumed, inept, indifferent.

Time went on with amazing and exciting rates. The seasons, with great moves.

Sometimes my own name cheered me up when I saw it on paper.

From the moment I saw horror, myself and myself were more or less strangers.

My actions were resistant to analysis and surveillance.

My body, at times, defective.

I could see it from my head and so there was no point in the clock or the mirror setting.

I thought I was living someone else's life, but had no idea whose.

HYPOSUBJECT

Yes, there were gardens in cities.

But we were lost in our course.

I thought I'd always known you. I thought my teeth to be cut from your teeth.

When the weather came, I heard the ground fall. I heard the net.

I opened my doors and wept.

It was the peak season. I was learning to cut fruit.

As new leaves grew, I was an invalid user.

I called to say your name outside a small window in the clouds.

Where I knew no one would hear me.

THE THIRD SPACE

At the end of the road
Is a space wide enough
That the far side
Is blurred in the heat
And it's hot
Though it's still June.
Still, we are gathered
Some are reading
Some garden
Or grill
In the square where grilling is legal
The margins of which are patrolled
Above which a plume
Of smoke rises
And across Columbiadamm
A basin gathers rain.
We forget this is a ruin.
We train cameras on each other.
We train cameras on the text
Projected in the mezzanine.
We pass around a fire
On the fire escape
And pinch the map
To see more clearly
Where it is we're going.
Things are not always
Only as they are.
If I'm speaking through a cracked
And smattered voice
It is my only speaking voice.
If I'm imitating how you speak
This is how I learned to speak.
A frantic architecture.
I mean, forensic architecture.

There is a wall here
Made of river rocks.
It stood here all these weeks
So quietly
Until I saw it.
Sometimes translation
Is revenge.
Someone who I loved
Once called dreams
The underwater theater show.
I mean, I lived with them.
I don't know I know
The difference.
The pommes by the lake were not
Cooked through.
It's true the reviews
Were pitiful
Though I only read them later.
The currywurst was only hot
On the outside
The bun stained
Like a pencil.
Stop only for emergencies.
On the far side of the lake
There was still sun
But we all got a bit sad
Though no one said it then
And the messages we sent
Describing where we were
Did not arrive until we left.
In this way the lake
Was latent.
Sometimes a friendship
Is untimely
A friendship
With the dead

As in the politically dead
Or the dead in the sense
Of an unfinished project.
An unfinished season.
A frenetic archive.
The numbers have faded.
What could be the reason
The curtains are closed?
A word for someone
Who doesn't speak the language.
A word for someone who tends the untended land.
A word for someone sleeping.
We are writing
A history of sleep.
The book predates itself.
If sleep is a place
Of reconstitution
I am unconstituted.
Sometimes living
Makes you sick.
A poisoning landscape.
A disappeared river.
Mining emotional futures.
Something has happened
And it is still happening.
Some of us come
From a bloodline of dissidents
And others of adherents.
But lineage is always plural.
I cannot contemplate
While I am waiting
And I am always waiting.
Still, there is a surplus
In the margins
To make this more sustainable.
Serena will bring cherries.

Maisa will bring
Caesar salad and Jalal Toufic.
I will bring the baby
And a cake of rye and cardamom.
This is different than
The old gaze of nostalgia.
To leave the event
And become the event
Go and take the little book
And eat it.
To speak from the stomach
Without the mouth.
To know with the liver.
To know with the little intestine.
No additional text.
We are here in the garden, early.
The show has not yet started.
The basin, after rain
Is ripe and sensitive.
For a few moments, two of us
Bear the weight of the bag together
For no particular reason
Heat where our skin is touching.
Time keeps coinciding
With itself.
If you take the words away
What you have left is a tree.
Now I will take out
The words.

torpor

BUSINESS

Once, I lived with a woman who became over time an important part of my life, though the day we sat to sign the binding contract at the Starbucks near Penn Station was the first time that we met

I had, shortly beforehand, typed her name into an image search in order to be certain I could pick her out among the crowds, predicting that the franchise would be large and busy, which it was

I was sweating as I sat between the woman and our landlord, sliding out my laptop from my backpack to rest it on the surface of the table, which was modular, designed to fit a range of changing needs, and open it to try again to move the sum that was demanded as deposit from my bank to the bank account belonging to the landlord

As its black screen lit, it was the grid of public domain images of Ariel that met our eyes

My eyes, the landlord's eyes, the eyes of Ariel.

∩

The first time, from the train, in the country where I live now, I saw the shanty-town of run-down shacks on the strip of land along the tracks, I wondered, as I've learned that many do, if my impressions of the country had been wrong

I was mistaken, for what I saw was not a shantytown but rather private plots of land for leisure, dotted with sheds, where people spent their weekends and their holidays, pruning thorny roses

Filling pails with cherries and tomatoes.

∩

At the time, I was beginning to acquire a new vocabulary for the names of baby clothes, receiving a heap of secondhand bodies and stramplers, which I washed and folded, then stacked in the drawer that had once held my socks

Songs in foreign languages I'd sung in childhood were playing in my brain, such as the song I sang each night at French Camp, sitting at the day's end, around a bonfire, which went, *Goodnight, goodnight wolves / The day is complete / All is still / Around the fire / Which says to us / Goodnight, goodnight wolves*

The lyrics of the song looped backward on themselves, beginning again, and again

The camp that I attended was expensive, a fact I only later came to be aware of, a cost that certainly was paid for by the portion of the fortune that my father had inherited from his grandfather, a garbage truck driver who'd climbed the ranks of the waste industry

Who died at the bank, his favorite place, after the golf course

His funeral, attended by a long parade of trucks designed to transport garbage

To his dump in Savage, Minnesota

Which had employed, during the summers, my teenaged father

The letters of his business emblazoned on the knit hat that I wore as a teen

BFI, later bought out by Waste Management, then merging with USA Waste Services, known initially as American Refuse Systems

A company that I assume never embraced the acronym ARS

Though *arse*, with its Germanic roots, was once considered a polite term for the buttocks

Refuse, a slightly formal word for waste, suggesting garbage on a very large scale

A word that shares a spelling with the verb *refuse*

Differing only in syllabic stress.

∩

Lately, in order to sleep, I need to listen to a podcast on the origins of English, the language

Playing, again and again, the episode about the word *Neanderthal*

A word coined in western Germany

A word named after a valley

A valley that, incredibly, lay mere hundreds of meters from the tracks the ICE took as I cut southward toward Köln

Where I sat in irritation, resenting, unjustly, the conversation of the white-haired woman seated in the row before me on the ICE toward Köln, though I had, earlier, engaged in animated talk with my companion for the duration of an hour

Though it was only later that I pieced this fact together, the location of the valley

Its proximity to me, in my state of irritation

A valley quarried for its limestone, vital for producing steel and iron

Blocks of earth gouged out and sold

It was strange to sell raw blocks of earth

Though, of course, it was a labor, mining.

∩

It was in the gouging of the valley that a trio of human remains was uncovered

Though upon examination, it was determined that the skeletons were *not* human

Belonging instead to a distinct and extinct species of archaic humans

The species was named after the valley

The valley named after Neander, a man descended from a man who'd changed his name from Neumann to Neander

Out of reverence, possibly misdirected, for the ancient Greeks

Both names meaning "new man"

I find, at times, the taste of my own mouth to be abhorrent.

∩

Now again, I was traversing the green breadth of a country, the one in which I live, if only newly, moving in a westerly direction on a train

I was traveling for business

My first business trip, my ticket and my hotel paid for by a company with limited liability

Ein Gesellschaft mit beschränkter Haftung

In partnership with the US embassy, with the aims to promote the culture of the country of my birth

A job for which I would later be paid by bank transfer

A sum, the lion's share of which I'd spend at Edeka, the largest supermarket corporation in the country where I live now

The name of which is an acronym in disguise, a phonetic elongating of the letters *EDK*, which stand for *Einkaufsgenossenschaft der Kolonialwarenhändler*

Or *Purchasing Cooperative of Colonial Goods Merchants*

The traces of its origins twice hidden

Lion's share, a phrase originating in a fable, in which the lesson is, explicitly, that a partnership with the powerful is never to be trusted

Partnership

Another kind of ship.

∩

It is Monday, the day that business can begin again and has begun

I wrote this in my notebook, oversized and spread before me at the breakfast buffet provided by the Motel One Köln-Messe, seated at a high-top from which I watched three businesspeople slip into the courtyard, where they sucked up vapor out of metal tubes that heated plugs of leaves from the tobacco plant, producing nicotine vapor without burning, a smoking without smoking

The space around me, filled with people speaking to their colleagues, chatter in a language I could mostly understand, if only on a word-to-word basis

Meaning, among the conversations at the Motel One Köln-Messe, I rarely encountered a word that didn't appear in my mind as a word, and yet the words did not cohere into meaning

The businesspeople, clad in muted tones designed not to be noticed, though I noticed them

I noticed, too, the two brown stains upon my once-white sneakers, where a stink bug, I believed, secreted liquid on me in the garden

The pants I wore, the only pants that I could wear now, elastic panel tight around my middle

My figure, full of baby

Baby's first business trip, I thought, as I picked out the English words among the German chatter

The night before, I'd dreamt the baby pressed its face against the inside of my body so hard that I could see its features through my skin

So that's what you look like, I thought, in the dream

The smokers, I noticed, were locked outside, inside the courtyard

I stood up to let them in, and one proclaimed me a *Lebensretter*

Though I'd saved no lives

I understood but in response could only say *kein Ding*

No thing

Nothing.

∩

The Motel One Köln-Messe brands itself a "budget design hotel," which aims to be aesthetically pleasing yet affordable, and arguably meets both of these aims

At the breakfast buffet, a well-hidden speaker plays tunes from my mother's childhood

A slow lilting cover of "Bella Ciao," with the protest wrung out

The melted revolution, background noise to pleasant chatter over muesli and the jetting of mechanically expressed coffees, bladders of milk somewhere in the back of the AutoBarista, connected by tubes to the frother

I, too, am here on business

Geschäftlich, we confirmed to the receptionist with consciously straight faces

A word, I think, that shares its root with *ship*

Freundschaft, Wirtschäft, Geschäft: there are many kinds of ships

But no, I later learn, I am mistaken; there is no common root between *schaft, schäft,* and *ship*

The suffix *shaft* and *ship* originate from the Old English *shape*, whereas *schäft* originates from the Germanic verb *to split* or *carve*

North of here, there are whole towns that seem to have no industry other than the selling of marzipan to tourists

Pounded sweetened almonds rolled into logs and dipped into chocolate, or formed to resemble tiny castles or potatoes

The city, still rich off the wealth it accrued centuries earlier, when the Hanseatic League exerted a monopoly on trade

Their business, the business of business

All business, the business of growth

All growth, an energy transfer

It never comes from nowhere

At the breakfast buffet, I carve slices of bread from an extremely long loaf that, ultimately, I do not eat

Everybody, now, a cheerful voice exhorts from the speakers.

∩

On the paper table mat before me was the hotel's slogan:
LIKE THE DESIGN, LOVE THE PRICE

From where I sat, before my plate of crusts, the spires of the Gothic Kölner Dom were visible

Through the chain-mail curtain hanging in the floor-to-ceiling windows of the foyer

The Kölner Dom, a church that took six centuries to complete

A church built on the ruins of six successive churches

The footprints of which lay under the cathedral

One spire, a few fingers taller than the other

A vestige of the time that has elapsed since their construction

The church's face, the largest in the world.

∩

The night before, Vanessa and I emerged from the bowels of Hauptbahnhof, where we were buying clementines and almonds from the all-night Rewe, anticipating hunger

Outside, we paused to look again, craning our heads upward, toward the Dom

Do you see, Vanessa said, they've just turned on the spotlights

Indeed, there was a golden light that fell now on the spires' upper reaches

Or is that sun? I proffered with uncertainty, for the hour was after nine and the sky was overcast

And yet, the light, unearthly

As if the mess of spires were glowing from within

We climbed the stairs and moved as if compelled to see the Dom's façade, searching all around us for a trace of any spotlight, finding none

None other than the sun, which, though we could not see it with our own eyes, seemed to have found a small window between the dark banks of clouds

The sun, simply going about its business

We stood still as the light turned red and then dimmed

Splayed on the church's façade.

BODY OF WATER 2

That spring, it took so long to start a thing

And then so long to end it

In the peaks and troughs of the market

And the supermarket

Where events that passed suggested that I might not really be there

Blocks of salted cheese kept disappearing from my cart

And when I thought that I was saying *whole* I was saying instead *pieces*

When I spoke with friends it was with distance and I heard their cities' sirens

When I woke it took place on the lines of a coordinate grid

And everywhere I went cement was being poured

Pumped up to a great height and then funneled back to earth

Trash blew past me on the day before Good Friday while I sat in the dirt on the banks of the canal

The path beside teeming with infants strapped tightly to the bodies of their parents

As if, in abject loneliness, some bodies had simply begun to bud.

△

I silenced my phone

I willed myself ill

I unmuted myself on the call, but when the goldenrod box appeared around my face I found I couldn't speak

And finally someone else piped in to tell the speaker she was muted

Though when the bells rang, I wanted, too, a rhythm

I wanted to ring with my own sound, to permeate space concentrically

I thought I should be grateful for my windows, with a view of two trees in a courtyard fenced off from me

But I only grew resentful I could hear the neighbor snoring

I watched as the light licked itself out, and then as it began to thicken

In increments of minutes.

△

All year, I conversed with myself through imagined conversations with the parents of the children whom I watched for money

Whose penthouse looked out across the flooded trench I loved

In my head, the parents asked me questions and I answered, composing my responses in increasing detail, in a mode I thought would charm them

Though, in real life, they rarely asked me questions

Instead I walked the city, a wet eye

Everything sticking to me

Or going right through

And at night, the streets light up with neon collars on the necks of dogs.

△

On the first warm day of spring, a car ran a red light on Pannierstraße and brushed
one hand of the child I watched as he slid into the crossing on his rollies

Provoking a chorus of screaming

His sister whispering afterward that if he'd died, at least she could have had his toys

And later, the uncle of the children introduced himself after he had watched me
watch the children at the playground for an hour

Suggesting I consider purchasing insurance, protecting me from liability in case of
harming others

Deliberately or not

Your name, the mother of the child once commented, how funny that it's really *yours*

I would have thought that it was yours from marriage.

△

What is the word, again, I ask on Zoom

A swollen spot on the roof of my mouth where it met my teeth.

△

On a public Zoom call my estranged lover turns her camera on and asks about the
journey down the river

And I watch her form her words, knowing she doesn't know I'm watching

And there is no way from here to reach her

In this city there are two of everything: two zoos, two airports, two operas

I, too, come from a twinned city, two cities that grew to form one

Though I guess it's not the same, merging and being bisected

Outside, the birds chirp like dial-up modems

Neon moss the color of the willow tree on the canal wall beneath the willow tree

Where a couple turns to face the wall until I pass

There is just a single word for *safe* and *sure* and *certain* in the language

What is loose flaps in the wind and I notice I'm wearing my sweater inside out and backward

Like I dressed in the dark, though I didn't

I notice I sleep with my head always turned to the left

I notice I hold my breath when I run

And everywhere I go, I see the strip of bricks denoting the wall whose absence is my age exactly

Its state of non-existence, the most permanent of states

The sidewalks populated by ergonomic strollers with lightweight aluminum bars

With weather-resistant fabrics and lightweight aluminum bars

Cradles with dark mouths so deep that often no baby can be seen

And sometimes the strollers really are empty.

△

In a book, a dot bleeds through the paper

That the pages might correspond with each other

Surface to surface, or uniquely bound by hyperlink

Though the screen seems to grow when it shows nothing at all, a will to overtake my field

Each day, I recombined seven letters to make known words, an addiction to distraction

Each day, I wore a sign of starker urgency

The still life begins to abscond

To self-disassemble and flee

In the gallery, a beating of the rising ocean

A punishment for mutability, susceptibility to change

The figs rise up, lifted by a flock of grapes

The string was strained and then soured

What good is empathy if it dead-ends in flesh?

My dot over a steep ridge in the watery red of evening

The forest filled with figures bent over their baskets, gathering wild garlic with a fever

And a sense that we would all bike home and pulverize the *Bärlauch* to make *Bärlauch* pesto

And still a lack of synchronicity, even with our bodies making shapes that rhymed.

△

My dot between two trees

My dot along the kidney-shaped body of water

And on the bridge, two children selling seed bombs

Balls of earth to throw at earth to make things grow.

VACUUM

"Imagine,"
began every page
of the book that the children I babysat asked me to read
screaming GOOD! and jumping on the bed
when they learned I could read English
we thought that you couldn't read English, they said
no, I can read English

Imagine living inside a potato
and cutting into a potato and finding a mark
believing the mark is a sign
from a power higher than you
and making it into a bumper sticker
as proof of God

Imagine an autumn with no leaf blowers
no men wielding leaf blowers at seven in the morning
and blowing the exhausted leaves, exhorting them to move
from a distance, aiming that long tube
much like a man imagines a higher power

When the children were finally asleep
after I practically held them down to brush their teeth
then scratched their backs, arms, legs, bellies, and heads
at their command, like I was a leaf, exhorted
they breathed so gently
suddenly entirely different animals

In the second book I'd read to them
an outcast wolf was forced to kneel
before a posse of rival wolf pups
press his face into the earth in submission
longing to be with his own kind
to know the names of the stars in his own wolf-tongue

I said I liked the word for vacuum cleaner
Staubsauger, because it means dust sucker
and *geschnitten*, which made my lover ask
if I liked it because I had recently cut off the tip of my finger
no one, he said, even knows what a vacuum means

The morning after the election, still thinking he had won
I went to La Maison with Carlos and Rebecca
and we all smoked rolled cigarettes with our croissants and cappuccinos
like we were role-playing Americans in Europe
sitting on a bench beside the bocce ball courts on the canal
even though we were just living

I lived for so long in a void, I said
in my private dissociation
I think, I said, we should take comfort
in the anarchy of our zigzagging life paths
a sort of haven from the hegemony of constant growth
which was pushed on us from all directions

I need to write to think, I thought
but whenever I sat down to write
I couldn't think

My mind, the British girl was always saying in German class, *has gone completely blank*
I tried to imagine that interior
we were discussing interiors
of apartments at all times
the number and size of rooms in apartments
and the rent if the rent roof were toppled

In German, I mix up *Sätze* and *sitzen*
sitting for long hours saying *Sätze*
listing the cases I know
stuck on the changes of the word *the*
according to a sentence's syntactical relations

I was crushing on my German teacher
who knew I was also a teacher
and came to me tenderly
at the end of the week to ask my advice
which I proffered
happy to be someone with anything to proffer

I brought cupcakes to class at the end of each week
vegan for Ali, for whom we used both *er* and *sie*
because there is no gender-neutral pronoun in the German language
and the word for *they* is the same as the word for *she*
as if there is a plurality to femininity
maybe there is

I was absurd; I celebrated
when a noun of the language was of my gender
as if I had a gender
as if I were a word

At the time I was building the future by mapping my period
by subtracting three days each month
projecting my blood on the ninth of November
as hypothetical and yet as certain
as a winner of a contest
or election

Complaints about the internet were spiking
we read on the internet
when ours sputtered out
we didn't know what to do without it; I could barely think
if I couldn't also Google
and so I decided just to read, which was different, entirely, from thinking—
more like living next to someone's thinking
and not like a machine
not like a machine at all

Perhaps the problem was that everyone was trying to find out
the same thing at once
though the information was often a *resolving host . . .*

I had hope, then, in that span of hours, for the Tongass Forest
the most vast of the vast Alaskan forests
a temperate jungle
which had been newly unbarred for logging
the loggers at its bounds, waiting to enter
and then begin the slashing

The blue bar of my browser crawled from left to right
and my organs at the core of me began to hurt
I was dreaming *oft* about having a baby
discussing at times with gravity
when and how
the main hurdle my monthslong fellowship
at a prestigious but isolated place
which had recently removed "colony" from its name

Oft means *often* in German
such a soft abbreviation, no tricks
it just means what it sounds like it means
like all of my favorites: *beenden, gewonnen, geschlossen*—

Zoé, my German *Cousine*
says German
is so easy, it's basically just English
English is German, she says
like two planets, I think, eclipsing each other
or formed from the same molten smatter

I was experiencing the pain of the body leaving the body
which always frightened me unduly
though it happened as oft as the full moon
I stayed up Googling pictures of uteri
in German, *die Gebärmutter*, the birth mother
its hollow pocket swollen pathologically by fibroids
or with graying patches, an illustration of endometriosis
to have a uterus is to know and to fear its diseases

On election night, I skipped the reading group
on moaning and mourning
and received instead the Loyalty Soul Award
for correctly identifying "suitcase" in the language
which I took to be an omen, a good omen
as for years I've dreamt recurrently of losing my luggage
or showing up for a very long trip without it

At night the beamer in my living room spits out light
illuminating the dust, some of which used to be my body
and I watch it, drifting, half-awake in my lover's uncle's bamboo rocker
then I look out the window, to the building opposite ours
where a cold white light is climbing, floor by floor, the stairwell
remaining lit for a minute
then zigzagging back out

ZEITGEIST

While trying to take
A passport photo
In the Treptower Park Center
I encountered
A *fatal error*
And my credit flashed
To zero
In the booth lit
By the blinking slot
Which ate my money
So I quit the mall
Walking counter
To the guidance
Of adhesive arrows
On the tile attempting
To enforce a one-way system
For the purpose of reducing
Face-to-face encounters.
I was fearful
Of my longing
To make children
For it was, I thought
Absurd to wish
A person into being.
EVERYWHERE IS SOMEWHERE
Said the poster
In the semi-autonomous region
Where I lived
For a spell
Before leaving.
That morning the neighbor had fainted
In his bathtub
Me, standing useless
In the stairwell

While my partner
Attended Manfred
In his weakened state
Though Manfred
By reports from other neighbors
Had roller-skated
Through the neighborhood
As recently as last year.
I wanted
To do nothing
But kick the piles
Of accumulating leaves
On the side streets
Branching off
From my street
Which was only mine
In the sense
That I lived there
On terms that were conditional.
I was so good
At my job
Which was nothing
As I had no job
And neither did anyone else.
We were applying ourselves
To the weather
To finishing one single thought
Per afternoon
To taking clothes
Down from the rack
Without leaving the socks
Stiffened like the leaves
Of this season
Refusing to let go.
I was pieces
And needed to be

My component parts
Wrapped up
In silk
So as to not auto-react.
I couldn't believe
We'd abided the loss
Of the last expanse of forest
Our active unprotection
Of that which we loved most
As if on the altar
The spirit
Was giving up spirit
In the temple
Of profit and growth.
I, too, was insatiable
And yet something
Was going awry.
I was incensed
By my feeds
And the wood
Which was fake
Which I'd expected
To be real.
I was longing
For abjection
For pressure on my neck
Or the permeating stink
Of the otters
River and sea
Who lived at the zoo.
Yes
I'd passed the year
On Zoom
Watching my own face
As I sipped water
Attempting a grace

Which I didn't possess
In real life
Sometimes pinning
The live image
Of the person whom
I most desired
On my screen.
The word of the year
Was *listless*.
Of course
The word for *time*
Was just the word for *tide*
Subjected to years
Of shifts
In the sounds
That make speech
And the shifting
Of tongue
Against teeth
In the mouths
Of the people
Speaking.

ONE THOUSAND NIGHTS

I dreamt of this, yes, of a city in weather

Another place where I am indecipherable

A pen with loose ink in my hand

When did I begin to have preferences?

And when did what I tended to draw nearer to begin to blur?

In the time since the internet was released for use beyond the US military

A crystallizing sense of self

Even as a new ease pervades the city, the horror of the painted vine atop the medical complex

Though the muted one

And from a balcony, a baby

And the small sound a person's body makes in the moment just before they speak

The sea, consisting of meter

Though my inability, when asked to explain what I mean by tone

As many nights as I have opened, I have closed

Sometimes the premise really is too much to bear.

~

Once, I had a lover who described the careful early touches as belonging to epistemology

A flat palm and investigative mode, which both excited and repulsed me

Here, infants in tights and fitted bonnets wander the streets like serfs gone small with age

At this fungible café

I feel myself a reptile

My little face reflected in between the endless stream of images that aim to hook me

How few words I manage to extrude.

~

Now the cherry blossoms wilt.

Now the chestnut blooms are wilting.

Now the azaleas are wilting.

Is that corn? Ali asks of grass that grows long on the street between us, and I break into cartoonish imitation of my native language.

~

Here, a man opens a beer with a beer while holding his phone to his ear with his shoulder while walking, every object and body in use

Already, spent leaves drift on the poured cement sidewalk, fungally spotted

This unuprootable habit of ending with *or*, a softening at the end of every sentence

Or, every sentence made exchangeable

Though my mother's mother's remains remain at the morgue

Though her death was in the summer, and again it's summer

Once, I was moved to great emotion by the last hours of a market on the last day of the year

Then everything else happened

The trees, I see, are thirsty, and I'd water them, but tonight there will be rain

I pant in hot excitement

I always say that I will stop this, but I do not, leading me to ask who it is commanding me

Or, how many of me are there?

I fear I

Though I've finally taken up art

I produce faint paintings and hang them before my tolerant partner, the jade

Furious rain in the wings

Against the hacking of the weed whacker, the neighbor plays piano

Sometimes I sing unconsciously and sometimes, from above, she echoes me

Though I've never met her

Though the other neighbor, housebound, rings us daily, and I go to pick up dark bread for her

And still, again and again, I become hole

How many words can you spell with seven letters?

I cradle my handy, on average, ninety-five times in a day, press my special whorl to it to open

Sesame

Open, sesame

That old phrase a French Antoine inserted into tales he pulled from Arabic and sold

A node of traveling stories on which, as it crossed the continents, new layers accrued

Sesame, meaning fatty seed, from the Akkadian *šamaššamu*

A crop grown at the margins where the other crops refused to grow

A seed that traveled as fast as language

A seed that rang exotically to European ears

When I search *the sesame seed*, I receive a local keto store

Sesame, open yourself

Thou buff, tan, or purple

Thou tubular flower, your four-lobed mouth

Wanton pod that bursts when ripe, resisting harvest, no wonder

I love you

The pod of me releasing my timed seeds in my very middle, familial gold around my neck

Sesame, open

Sesame, sesame, close.

mortar, pestle

THE FIRST PLANETARY BOUNDARY

For the important thing is time.
Handshakes and conflicts,
including genders and ramps
from the future and all other times
as well. Naturally, between and unseeing,
I went through all the numbers' centers:
hand, foot, mouth; smoke
in and out. No need for paradigmatic
gymnastics. Dramatic.
Already, the Amazon has burned out;
there is five of everything.
The compact elements adorning
the plenum, complaining
in heterogeneous fashion of infection.

THE SECOND PLANETARY BOUNDARY

Items were there and removed
without ever leaving me.
Sex, inscribed with a certain roteness.
In fact, I was very remote at all moments.
In every new being, the past.
This turned out to be wrong.
All these zooming processes
of future, they exhaust me.
This whole thing, awakening
my secret fault. But the day is almost over.
Me? I am tired. I awoke
in a glacier, which I could feel
was hungry for my body.

THE THIRD PLANETARY BOUNDARY

Cool data streams were happening
to everything on earth and everything
beneath it. Surfactants, keeping boundaries
lubed and fluid, and the economy,
of course, running at peak.
At every precipice, a narrow memory:
a harrowing road, a hammock in the sun,
a reptile in a box. A straw home,
a wood home, a stone home;
each has lost its value indefinitely,
and the landscape, prone and ripening,
becoming obscured with debris.
The debris, singing the song, leaning forward
by means of classical machines.

THE FOURTH PLANETARY BOUNDARY

They finished the song
one by one: panopolis, ellipsis,
local affairs; all of us insatiable
despite the logos and its thick
pleasure. No, I can do nothing
about the lawn. But it doesn't worry me,
really. I am ready to reproduce,
and I know that I shall.
Of course, my heart, a little tight again,
and my body, resting on property.
My sex monitored by frostbite,
latex, rind. Profligate and flaze,
glistening in the hole that was me
and my body. Look, they said, it's magic.

THE FIFTH PLANETARY BOUNDARY

In fact it was only ordinary sorcery,
but I had always been thus gifted.
Guaranteed, I drove my silver van
of speculative worth, the contract
comprised of value alloyed from lesser value
but nevertheless not nothing.
There was enough lust
to oxidize fully by nightfall.
My money, small and subjected
to new terms, though elsewhere
abundant and growing in various oils
and accounts. Everything, so gilded
and indelible, conditions all more sculptural
than I remembered from last time.

THE SIXTH PLANETARY BOUNDARY

It was more scripted, less radiant;
more coveted, less noble;
more real, less formal;
more genealogical, less glittery;
more shining, more wide,
more crowded, more veering,
soon to be subject.
It did not yet, however, arise.
Yet to hear it was intoxicating.
Yes, yes, I was ultra-lush.
I was slushing around in my slush.
Who could understand such a thing?
I had been trained my whole life
for this wanting.

THE SEVENTH PLANETARY BOUNDARY

Self-loosened and set aside,
the database is crumbling.
This is no hands-on experiment.
The start was laughing at us;
my present company, a sullen gnat
and my dear self,
surfeit with desire
for non-derivative pleasure
which nothing could satisfy.
But soon I will come.
Everything, changed into value
in sight of wealth and travel.
Unknown in the state
of the subject.

THE EIGHTH PLANETARY BOUNDARY

Medium-long, long, and very long;
middle world stages are over:
a rib-roast temporality and in-built
arche, the old cult of alchemy.
I had already chosen my body.
It was wet for my wetness,
all the body I could handle,
beside myself at noon,
though I may have been
just a puff of blue above my belly.
Wounds put me on the table,
marked me with the rust of dandelions,
the bird cast out on either side of song.
Every summer, the same song.

THE NINTH PLANETARY BOUNDARY

The laminate floors pressing up
through my soles, and outside,
an ideal merging of land and aqua.
Your doubleness plus my doubleness
equaling a hot quadrupleness.
I was pretty good
when I was put into the world
all at once. The floors and I, of course,
contemporaries. The essence
of the lettered bit, distilled
into a wisp. Combination,
ripe and falling from the tree
of procreation, which was
the great art of knowing, more or less.

THE TENTH PLANETARY BOUNDARY

I was melting in the August sun.
The codex drooling, and little old me?
I was condensing my hardware
and software, my fingers a code
and immersed in a brine,
the tidepool of permanent change.
There were not unlimited nightfalls,
which astonished me. A scarcity
of future despite all history of synthesis.
Informatics; gross conditions
of material surroundings; the rise
of molecular motion; the brimming oceans;
and the sum of tenderness:
I was there. There I was.

portal

RADICALITY

For months, I've felt I'm not myself but my self's assistant, toiling on my self's behalf, half-here, half-nowhere as I plow through emails to my self's relatives and contacts.

I email my grandfather to say I peeled and cubed the quinces from the tree in his new wife's ex-husband's home among the redwoods, where he moved at ninety-two because he was too old to live in Kurdistan anymore, in these times.

The quince was green and white and shaped like a pear, but it wasn't a pear.

In this life, at night, I find I choose to scrape the meat of my attention on a grater so it tatters, disappearing into ether. Into the nether of the internet.

The internet thinks I want to have a baby, and I do.

It knows I ordered sticks in bulk to dip in pee to see what is happening in me, and everything else. We wanted it, panopticon in which we split to be both watched and watcher.

The first time I saw the *o* missing from *god*, I was ten and rendered speechless.

I had recently received a failing grade on a test of the ten commandments. I was raised to be skeptic by skeptics but believed in believing.

I believed in circles, in the potency of future, in holes between places and times. I know I know nothing wholly and will not. I didn't know where I came from but knew I would know its pitch and tenor when I heard it. And I hear it.

What should I say? There is a part of me that isn't me.

What I thought was rain on my roof was the kettle, warming. What I thought was a pile of rocks on the far spit of sand was a young whale, strangled in a fishing net and starved. What I thought was morning was twenty minutes past noon.

The tide was rising and I was late to my meeting with no one.

The young humpback was gray and white where its skin had come off, which it had, revealing what looked like some sort of foam. I wished to believe that the whale was a prop on a set about human catastrophe, but it wasn't. Or, this was the set, and we were all in it.

The stench was very strong.

The body of the whale would take a while to decay.

The hard white flesh of quince turned ruby as I boiled it down with sugar into jam.

We need to think about things a little more radically.

When the self finally appears, don't turn the self away.

NIHILISM

The week that I arrived there was an outbreak, which put us all on edge, and I woke up with jagged breath at each night's middle, wailing to my metal box which pinged my wails across the ocean.

The tide filled and emptied the basins around me twice daily.

The hourglass of sand I ordered on the internet arrived on time, and the days passed calendrically.

I read *A Field Guide to Cape Cod* and trod lightly on the lichen, which I knew my feet were capable of killing. One night, globs of algae washed up, pulsing with their own dim light.

I hadn't meant to let in the part of me that hated me, but there it was, hovering above my folded body in the attic that was, for a spell, my home.

I flew across the ocean, and when I came back, I could no longer sleep.

Something foreign had lodged in me and formed a cord, leeching from me what it needed.

A storm came and knocked out the power, then another. We all got sick, then recovered. An absence watched me as I lay in bed all day, rubbing my belly where I thought it might be.

Then sound, at frequencies too high to hear, was pulsed into my abdomen, reflecting back a mass that quivered in space with regular rhythm, a beating preceding an actual heart.

What is the point of flowers, a child had asked his mother last summer while I was bussing tables, lingering over smeary plates to eavesdrop on her answer.

The roses which proffer odd blossoms all winter here in the dunes of the cape came as cargo, stashed on a passenger ship heading to Boston from England that foundered and wrecked in fair weather the first day of March in the middle of a century of revolution, empire, and collapse. Driven ashore, the boat broke apart, discharging its cargo of nutmeg and linens and nursery stock, drowning some dozens, including the captain, who had conspired, it later came out, to sink the ship, doubly insured, worth more sunk than afloat.

A man who would lose his five daughters pulled the damning letters from a suitcase. Then gathered and planted the pear and plum seedlings cast up by the sea, a wrecker's garden.

The roses took root all on their own and spread along the cape's long arm, invasive.

The point of flowers, the mother had explained with a surgeon's precision, is to lure in bees, which pollinate the flowers so the flowers can make more flowers. Yes, the child replied, but what's the *point*, and I saw the seeds of a nihilism with which I was once well acquainted.

It's foolish, I think, to think that you know what you want.

DESTINY

That year was the year your mask left lines on your face which I wanted to trace with my fingers, though mostly, they faded untouched.

I talked you into it, then booked the Super Express deal on a website with five stars: marryabroadsimply.com.

We took the train to Denmark and afterward flew to the country in which I was born and traversed it, staying along the way in homes of friends and relatives, no home similar to the last, except the brand of hand soap, which everyone across twelve states seemed to prefer.

Lavender. Lemon Nirvana.

Everything else was shifting, the era unsteady. My friends' fortunes were diverging, and our trip felt like a tour of ways to live, like walking through the maze of showrooms at IKEA, except each home contained someone's one life.

My throat grew sore from so much talking, explaining in each state how we had met, a narrative that grew bulky under its own weight by the time we reached Cape Cod, where at dusk, I mistook a traffic light for the moon and gasped before I realized my error.

Once, I'd thought destiny a sort of room that you entered.

Bliss, or misery, another.

But sometimes my life really feels like my life.

All winter, I thought of Sky Barbara, the firstborn child of friends of friends I'd never meet.

I watched, on screen, a baby born *en caul*, asleep until a blue-gloved finger pushes through the sac and animates the body.

I generated faces of people that didn't exist and found that I already loved them.

One day, I walked a thin spit of land between two tidal basins and felt something coming.

Someone inside me that wanted to see what I saw.

The day we wed, strangers passing called to us in Danish from their bicycles, but we couldn't be sure of what it was they said.

The words hung in the summer blue for a breath, and then fled.

ABUNDANCE

Once, this was an island

And this was a flourishing river

Before it was stopped up

This year, they're undamming the river

One hundred years after its damming

But of course no one knows what will happen

Yeah, this place was settled by humans a very long time ago

Ten thousand years, give or take

They were out on the island

Then the colonists came

Houses were floated down the river

Then the land was bought

And a village was built in the style of colonial Vermont

I'm not sure exactly why

No, we're still on Cape Cod

What I mean is that this used to be an actual village

Now, it's a replica village.

∴

The prickly pear here is smaller than the prickly pears that grow in the Southwest

But they're still edible

Yeah, we're stuck in this scarcity narrative

But it falls apart pretty quickly

Farms are the source of food, we think

But food is all around us

Acorns were once the basis of starch in this region

Though we've lost the American chestnut

A blight arrived and wiped them out

And the trees that remained were cut down

At present, we have no American chestnuts.

∴

But acorns we have in abundance

Acorns were the basis for a lot of life for thousands of years

A lot of variety, too

We have white oaks, red oaks, English oak

Acorns are ripe for a comeback

White oaks germinate in fall

Their acorns are almost pure starch

Red oaks are the ones with pointy leaves

White oaks are the ones with rounded leaves

Red oaks don't germinate until spring

Their acorns are higher in fats and oils

Higher in nutritional value

And tannins are natural preservatives

So the acorns don't go bad

But sometimes they have weevils

Really cute little worms

They lay eggs in green acorns

And when they hatch they eat the acorn and fill it with poop

An acorn with a cap means the cap is cemented by weevil damage

English oak has distinctively long, thin acorns

Acorns . . .

Sort of a combination of flour and olives

But the tannins need to be leached before they can be eaten

If you took a bite now, you'd find them very bitter

But tannins are water soluble

Leach them in changes of cold water

Hot water would denature some of the enzymes that make up a starch

It takes some work

But it isn't totally dissimilar to other grains

You can make a sort of jelly

Or something like oatmeal

Or flour

So, let's walk.

∴

There are beach plums in August and maybe September

And dewberries, which look like blackberries

Rose hip tomato paste

It's getting a little late

The end of harvest season

Beach plums burst into bright white blossoms near the branch

And same with elderberries

Umbrella flowers

Blackberries, blueberries, late July and early August

Sometimes in the same areas as cranberries

A berry for the birds

There are cherries, wild cherries

The bark of cherry can be used to make a medicine for coughs

See the telltale bark: lenticels make stripes of white

Whereas the beach plum has tinier white stripes

Bitter, hardy oranges

You can make a marmalade

Grape leaves, currants

Grapes are native, will often overgrow whole areas

Fox grapes, wild holly

Mugwort, very common, a weed that grows everywhere

This is stinging nettle

They'll look almost purply in spring

They make a really good pesto

But take care when you harvest; you need a good pair of gloves

Wild onions, onion grass

Curly in the springtime

Looks like crabgrass and likes to grow with wild nettles

Often grows with wild nettles

Oh, and pin oaks

Smaller acorns with an oranger flesh

Which means more beta-carotene and oil

This is the oldest house still standing on this land.

∴

The flowers here are edible

Black locust tastes like cucumber

In June, May, the blossoms start falling like snow

Sometimes the ground can tell you more than the tree

Black walnuts look like big green oranges

But inside is a walnut

With a very black shell

And these berries you can boil and skim the wax to make wax candles

Hog cranberry, bearberry

But it takes a very lot of berries

Scrub oaks have acorns only if they are mature enough

They have a harsh life out here in the dunes

Stunted by the conditions

These are beach peas

You can sauté the tendrils in April

The younger they are, the more tender.

∴

Yeah, damming the river nearly wiped out all the herring

The herring here are born in the freshwater ponds

They still spawn

Swim out to sea and return

The fish have an instinct to swim back to where they were born

Back to the body of water in which they were spawned

And when the river was dammed, they were hit very hard

Soon, they will begin the process of undamming

We're cautiously optimistic

Though there are many unknowns

It's easier to dam a river than undam it

There used to be shellfish beds at the mouth of the river

There used to be oysters the size of small plates

Once, people caught bass in this river

But the bass don't come if there's nothing to eat

No

People don't catch fish here like they used to.

LUNCH

I sit on the Panke, its masses of green seaweed waving

Anchored in its shallow but swift-moving waters, said to be the fastest river in the city

Which looks almost viscous, thick with the early summer fluff jettisoned by trees

Though, is it really a river?

Trash floats past me, as if on a conveyor belt: a juice box, a foil bag, a sauce cup

Litter on a tour of the city

While I watch, a breeze disturbs my tiny empty packet of wasabi

Carrying it aloft and then into the water

The packet moving downstream with sudden purpose

I glance alarmed to see if anyone has witnessed

But they haven't

The couple nearest me discussing with intent whether to fly to Lisbon or Madrid

What are the two who've appeared with buckets doing?

Maybe they dropped something into these waters, on which a pink flower now passes

They climb in the shallow water, among the masses of dense green leaves

They are fishing out the weeds

They are putting the weeds in their buckets

What will they do with them?

To where will they convey the weeds hauled from the Panke, and for what purpose?

The brown duck, too, buries her head and fishes about for food

Me, I have eaten my fill

ALPHABET

When my space bar breaks, I notice the keys on my keyboard have worn where I've touched them

A tiny white hole like an ulcer where my thumb must rest

The S, C, B, M, and L keys obscured by wear

Why not the most common letters? E, T, A, and I remain unmarred

It's a mystery, but I imagine

It has to do with the angle at which my fingers hit the keys

It's hard to write without a working space bar, with no space between each word

It's true I am a sort of violent typer

Really pounding at the letters

A day after I fix the space bar by shaking out my laptop, the T key comes off

I am able to put it back on

It stays on

Later it falls off again

Then again

Eventually I put it back on upside down

This seems to do the trick

BEACH

The mocha really was as good as I'd imagined

My resentment for small dogs still constant

The bird cry really sounded like a child

May you have a blessed day, the woman whose voice was a rock in my shoe said to strangers

People trading tips on the best vacation places while vacationing

We were all complicit in this tangle

I wasn't confused, just annoyed that not everything was going exactly according to plan

I wished for the season to be over, meaning, tourists

I wanted it empty

It was Sunday

Hopefully they would all leave and take their chatter elsewhere

I couldn't handle blather

"Very fun," one half of the couple was repeating

Projecting her voice impressively over the sounds of the ocean

No, the crying was really a baby

Some people don't know when to stop

I will never own a dog

Definitely, they all insisted multiple times, apropos of their keeping in touch

Finally, they parted

What I wanted was total silence

Too many species gathered on this shore, all of them overly vocal

The speaking woman continuing to make kissy noises to her captive creature

Then carrying him down the stairs, which he could not manage alone

It did feel good admittedly to be out in the world, even if it was all gritty and scratched me

I felt like a person again

A woman hushing Skyler, whom I wondered, child or dog?

I calculated the odds of having a daughter, as if gender were real

Noting the sons of my friends, as if that were how chance worked

I'd dreamt I'd had two sons, exactly as I'd hoped not to

Though once, as a younger person, I would have said I'd rather parent boys than girls

I'd had such a bad girlhood once I was no longer seen as a child

I didn't know how to act, feel, see, or be, and nobody told me

I thought myself wholly devoid

Actually, I like to come and spend mornings outside at the bay

Despite the constant clang of buildings being built

I need to buy a winter jacket

Write a poem about stampedes

Write Neil and Cheswayo

Send one million emails

Humidify my home, so I don't dry of dryness

I'm gonna be totally okay

Maybe buy two jackets

I'm going to be just fine

INTERNET

I watch a blurry video of oil, ink-like, spurt up from floor tiles while a man withdraws his money from an automatic teller.

After the storm, I step on a buried bird at the beach. Soft as a loaf of bread.

As the raw of dawn develops, I hear the alarms of others. Metal against metal.

Everywhere I go, I click Agree, consent to cookies.

I post an image of the old Tostitos jar I found washed up on the beach, MILD AND CHUNKY, rusted lid still holding in gray liquid, and the violinist I met years ago in Montreal, the one with the secretly Kurdish grandfather, writes me.

Open it, he says. Says, it clearly wants to merge with something bigger.

The website says it hopes to continue to exchange as much information with me as possible.

The earrings came to me on accident, addressed to Mary Gooden but stuck in the fold of my mail. Hoops of false silver sent from the Gulf, and I never send them back.

When the avocado was ascendant, doctors saw a sharp rise in wounds to the palm. I read it somewhere: the fruit in the hand, the blade through its skin into skin.

The cold, for now, has frozen all the sand in place, and I can tell my own tracks from the others in the dunescape from the way my feet point outward. A sort of private network.

Outside my window, Laura stands half in, half out, dumping sand out of her boots.

Who will pore over my traces when I'm gone?

Iraq, I try, when the doctor asks where I'd been living and Kurdistan won't register.

Iraq, I say, Iraq? And finally I say it how I know she'll understand.

She points to where my waves jump seismically and says, see this? Your brain is getting a little squirrelly here.

And confirms this as potential origin of brain fog.

Eartha's pixelated repost reads:

YOU ARE NOT READING THIS
BY ACCIDENT
THIS IS YOUR SIGN THAT EVERYTHING
IS GOING TO BE ALRIGHT.

CHANGE

Somewhere in my body was a body.

The year was whittled down to weeks when I found out.

The year was the year I had published a book, which isn't the same as writing one and worse.

When I read from it before the public, it was in a Zoom room.

It was my own face that I saw as I read, my own eyes that my eyes met.

The cover of the book was a distorted face, and that is how my body felt, too: in pixels.

I felt I had more blood in me. My dogtooth ached when I drank hot tea.

My cells felt magnetized and also very banal. A new freckle on my nipple.

Baby doesn't like, I started saying when the drilling of the new deck went on and on.

Baby likes, I said when I liked anything.

The source of all change, a pregnant emptiness. According to the poets.

On the internet, I watched a woman style her hair in 500 years of hairstyles, totally gripped.

Songs I hadn't heard in years appeared in my mind, and when I played them, I wept.

And I wept when I read of a child's capacity for grief.

And I wept when I watched pony rehab.

My body, so body, recited the poet's daughter.

My body. And my not-body.

WORM

I wasn't waiting my whole life for you.
But now, when I write, I write mostly in your anticipation.

Mostly, I call you worm.
Moving underneath the surface, hypothetical until it floods.

Not a copy, mold, or echo.
Not made against the shape of something else or reverberated off a surface.

More body flooding out of body.
More composite: two planets, smashing together.

For example, the taxi leaving my ancestral town.
So recklessly I leapt out halfway to the capital.

For example, a novel and virulent agent, growing as my love grew.
Reprogramming the honeycomb of living things to do its replication.

Yes, for you to live, non-living things.
And semi-living things that spread and made the living cease to live.

Worm, from the hypothetical root *wer-*, to turn, to bend.
As in *verse*, to turn back. As in the German *werden*, to become.

Or Old English *wyrd* for fate, for what befalls one.
Or *warp*, or *wring*, or *worth*. Or *reverberate*. Or *converge*.

Yes, at first you'll be unseeing.
For half a year, you'll know only my body's single taste.

Then you'll encounter the world.
The world will flood in.

And the world will keep flooding in.

GONG

I have exhaled
Fricatives percussively
Observing the weak drum
Of my abdomen
Bellowing
In the mirror
To reactivate
The muscles
Which hold in
My organs.
I have imagined
The rootlets
Of new nerves
Extending
To carry sensation
Back to the crescent
Of numbness
Above the line
That marks the boundary
Of no dimension
In between us.
Sometimes I love best
When I can't see
What I am loving
When I am
Away from you
One morning
In November
On the bridge that spans
The artificial waterway
Which was once
A drainage ditch
And then an ersatz route
For boat traffic

A shallow channel
Into which the body
Of Rosa Luxemburg
Was thrown
Though today
The water is
Primarily a site
Of recreation
Where at present
I was sipping
When my eyes
Locked with the eyes
Of someone else's child
Moving pliantly
Back-first
Into the future
Just like I do
Permanently turned against
The substance
I am moving through
Scrolling backward
Through the weeks
To bring myself
Up to the present.
The problem is
That everything
Has been shellacked
At its own limit
With a varnish
Mediating
All relation
Meaning that I am unable
To actually see you
Even as your tiny fingers
Claw at me
And mark me

With tiny lacerations.
Shellac comes from
The lac bug
A resin that collects
On the twigs
Of a plum tree
Or palash
Excreted through the pores
Of limbless female insects
Who burrow
In the bark
As they produce
Their many eggs
Completing two full life cycles
Each year.
The twigs are harvested
By cutting
Then crushed
Between two iron wheels
To harvest the resin
Which is sifted and heated
And pulled into sheets
Then dissolved in a solvent
And sold.
I only hear the ringing
Certain mornings
Of the bells
Which mark the hour
On the weekends
Though the weeks
Are endless
If unmarked
By scheduled labor
Days slack around my ankles
Gathering concentrically
Around the soft form

Of your body
Like a tree
Producing new growth
In the cambium
At the trunk's periphery
Each tree's infancy
Inscribed at its true center
Meeting each new year
Completely bare.
Other days
It seems the air
Stands dumbed.
Are bells gongs?
Are gongs bells?
Some instruments
Just will themselves
To earth.
The flute carved
From a thigh bone
Unearthed from deep
Within the caves
Of modern-day Slovenia.
And the triangle.
Idiophones
Whose bodies oscillate
Around a point
Of equilibrium
Ringing with
Indefinite pitch.
What emotion has
The highest frequency?
What is
My normal mode?
Keep in mind
This isn't science.
When you came

The bells were still
Suspended
In their towers
The sun also suspended
In the darkness
Of official night
Its geometric center
Eighteen degrees
Beneath the line
Of the horizon
Inching upward
Through the twilights
Nautical and civil
Then it dawned
On us
And everything
And rung and rung.

BIRTH

You were born in a brutalist building.
Rising above a long body of water.
The body, a bypass canal.

You were born beneath six beaming spotlights.
Born of a sharpness, and set to music.
In the backroom, on a tablet, through a portal.

A glory, a watermark's scar.
And with a great whoosh, Orlando.
Orlando, known by the land.

And the unbowing was there.
And the ecstatic, a humming.
And a great sorrow was there.

ACKNOWLEDGEMENTS

So many of these poems found their final form in workshops, correspondences, and shared documents with friends, whose brilliance and camaraderie are what makes all this fun and sustainable. I'm so happy to know you all. Thank you especially to Ariel Yelen, Elijah Jackson, Kelsi Lindus, Laura Cresté, Patty Nash, and Renata Ament for reading so many of these poems and often at short notice. Thank you too to Sterling HolyWhiteMountain for talking writing with me, and much love to my Kurdish Poets' Collective, Hajjar Baban, Holly Mason Badra, and Pınar Yaşar. A special thank you to Brenda Shaughnessy for fielding my late-night panic emails, and always being in my corner. And a huge thank you to Ben Mauk and Carleen Coulter for giving me and my poetry a home in Berlin at the Berlin Writers' Workshop.

I am so grateful to the editors of this series, Douglas Kearney, Katie Peterson, Rosa Alcalá, and especially Srikanth "Chicu" Reddy, for believing in this project and ushering it into the world. Thanks, too, to Adrienne Meyers, David Olsen, Alan Thomas, and Lily Sadowsky at the University of Chicago Press for your generosity and care with *PORTAL*. I was only able to write and edit these poems in relative peace because of the fellowships and grants I received from the Provincetown Fine Arts Work Center, the Berlin Senate, and the National Endowment for the Arts. Thank you for your vital work in supporting the arts.

Thank you to the editors of the following journals, in which versions of some of these poems first appeared:

Bennington Review: "Radicality"

Ecotone: "Nihilism" (as "Cape Cod")

Forever Magazine: "The First Planetary Boundary," "The Second Planetary Boundary," "The Third Planetary Boundary," "The Fourth Planetary Boundary," "The Fifth Planetary Boundary," "The Sixth Planetary Boundary," "The Seventh Planetary Boundary," "The Eighth Planetary Boundary," "The Ninth Planetary Boundary," and "The Tenth Planetary Boundary"

Mercury Firs: "Body of Water 2"

Nowruz Journal: "One Thousand Nights"

Paperbag: the seven poems titled "Hyposubject"

Paris Review: "Birth"

Prelude: "The Third Space"

Southeast Review: "Internet" and "Change"

Yale Review: "Worm"

The poems "Body of Water 2," "Vacuum," "Zeitgeist," and "One Thousand Nights" appeared in a small-edition pamphlet published in 2022 by Dock 11 & Dock Art.

An enormous thank you to everyone who read *about:blank* and shared their support with me. That was more vital than you probably know, sustaining me through the difficult last years and making this book possible in so many ways.

Thank you to my parents. And thank you, most of all, to my other T, for really seeing me, and for creating time in a year with no time so I could finish this project.